edging

poems by Claire Evans

ARCANA
POETRY PRESS

This collection is dedicated to everyone who has supported my crazy alter ego, from friends who workshopped my pieces to family members who bought me new chokers... and Taylor Swift.

CONTENTS

anchored

like the buoy between your legs

pendulum swings / loud and clear

like menstrual blood

boiling over / into ecstasy

slick down my thighs

like teeth against your neck

stamp bruises / on party favors

like veins buried to the hilt

muscles quake / keep your pace

like fingers call my ocean

typewriter tips / taste salt and lonely

a six-inch sea

you were goosebumps in a hot bath
not deep enough / to submerge
so I sink one body part in at a time

the backs of my arms / your hands once held
shoulder muscles soothed like the soil
in our ceramic succulent pot / grateful
for a single drop of sustenance

my legs / once wrapped around your waist
knees buckled from holding out hope
like the dreamcatcher above my bed / patient
even when the sandman washes out

the curve of my belly and breasts / surfaced once
torso turned toward comfort
like the sunflowers outside your house / bright
but subject to overwatering

can a shallow hot spring heal me
one sin-soaked inch / at a time?

black, white, and wet all over

He keeps a perfect little tea cup
balanced on his knee / a wretched little
cigarette between his fingers / a smutty
little smirk on his lips—he wants to
know why my smile is a waxing crescent
with a shaking head and trembling
thighs, a portrait of anticipation.

We have realized we're both playing
the same game—seated on either side
of a thrift-store board / pretending our pieces
are ivory, not bone—wondering
who will hit the stop clock first.

I crawl across the table / scatter pawns
like inhibitions / plant myself
in his lap / shove my tongue down
his throat—he chuckles like he won,
but I'm here to flip the odds.

The drops of my desire are long past
boiling point—I'm spilling past
the rim / swelling up over the horizon
of insignificance / waiting to cascade
between the rocks of this carefully crafted
catastrophe we have built.

lips and teeth

I'll let you taste
the drops, my love,
but you can't take
the flow

uncork me at your
own risk—I'm shaken
champagne
in a white t-shirt

red lace stretches
across my panty line;
a steel bow holds
the scraps

I'll finger the cord
around your neck,
but you won't
withstand the fall

I met an older you and I loved him too

Did you know I met your soul again? Odd, because you're still here. I didn't think a soul could be split between two bodies in the same timeline, but look at you. You've found me again, my love. First in a high school gymnasium, telling me how much you hate pep rallies. Now across the ocean, with an ex-wife and an accent and a dozen years on me. It's you, though; I'm positive. You're still unattainable, not the kind of man any woman should fall in love with. You chased a girl from grade school through university, finally captured her, and built a life in the tiny house on her parents' property. Then she left, a flight of fancy to bigger and better things, while your feet stayed on the ground because you never learned how to tether yourself to someone else. Now you're alone and broken, like you always were, and I've somehow stumbled back into your orbit like some minor goddess trying to mend a string the fates have already cut. I never meant to be a seamstress. I never meant to touch back down on your shores. I never meant to see you again. But here I am, trying to touch my tongue to a soul that's just as stunted as it ever was. I could curl into this older you. Fall for him. Fuck him. Feel the cracks in his heart to see how much they've grown since your boyhood. It wouldn't matter. Knowing you in this lifetime means I've known you in every lifetime, and every single one of you has destroyed me.

It's a shame… another damn shame…

divine purpose

emotional

support

something-or-other

everyone wants to be something

but I guess my real value

lies in nothingness / I'm real

damn good at being

the void people scream into

how nice for them to know

they're someone's muse / to

dip their fingers in liquid onyx

and emerge unscathed

if only their fingerprints didn't linger

cold coffee case files

Take us back to the confession
where you said it all went wrong.
Give us every wounded word.
Turn your trauma inside out.

We want your exes and ecstasy,
every gasp you've ever faked.
Take the grain of salt to court.
Plead the fifth to let it fester.

Wait out the poison.
Turn the legal pads bloody.
Tell us how much it hurt
lighting torches on wet wood.

We want secrets whispered
in the damp of cum-soaked sheets,
before your bare feet hit the floor
to find the coffee already cold.

Scratch his indiscretions
on immortal steno screens.
Beat heartbreak like a plea bargain.
Steal the last word
and the high road.

bloody cuticles

My friends always notice

how healthy I look

when we're not on speaking terms

I wonder if her cuticles will bleed too

as she claws her way from

one-time booty call

to once-in-a-while friendship

to wonder-if-he-hates-me Instagram stalker

Maybe I'm not doing myself

any favors clinging to you

like you might have cared too

but you left me poems in pieces

stale breadcrumbs that led to nowhere—I guess

I was always hungrier than you,

more overcome by the taste—

a vampire with a full stomach and still-empty reflection

I'm sorry I let my longing show

didn't commit to knowing better

thought myself bold enough

to ask about your day

and wish you well

just let me fix my manicure

and remind myself that

scratches left on shadows

mean nothing

I won't set the table anymore

The day will come when I no longer starve for you. When I no longer hide between aisles in the grocery store because I heard you were back in town. When my lips no longer press against your name like flower petals stored in the pages of Bible prophecies. When my fingers no longer type cryptic notes down rabbit holes, leaving digital breadcrumbs in a vain attempt to stitch my soul into secret dreams between your sheets. I hope you feel the ache of that loss. May your lips dry bloody without the ichor of my pixel pen to praise the passing fad of your precarious promises. May your hands cramp around your desire, unable to pry her name from your throat because the echoes of mine aren't there to chase it with nostalgia. May the amber you always wanted oxidize like rust, your lungs gasping for the coffee-colored vapors you once knew better than your own whiskey. May the wings you watched me grow shed feathers of regret down your spine and plant tantalic notes in the ghost of your piano keys. May your eyes search every darkened corner, waiting for a match that will no longer catch. May your fingertips miss the wax that dripped under tables, through parchment seams, and down the nape of your neck back when your hair was still long enough to hold my fingers.

I hope your stomach churns as you discover what it means to hunger for a feast that is no longer laid out for you.

call me needy

Call me cling-wrap for the way my legs

wind around your neck. / Call me fickle

for the way I sent him home

with your leftovers.

***

Call me naïve for the way I cradled your

heart even knowing it was barely-there

and broken. / Call me psychic

for the way I carried band-aids

just in case.

***

Call me sunshine for the way I turn cheeks

pink and make tree trunks stretch to touch

my skies. / Call me storm cloud

for swelling your soil

with something sinful.

***

Call me breadcrumbs for the way I scatter

pieces of myself and wait for you to want

a taste. / Call me whiskey for the way

I want to burn, choke, and make

your throat close.

***

Call me Jackson Pollock for the way

I'd lay bare and let you paint me. / Call me

Icarus for the way I'd coat my feathers

in your wax.

fuck dignity

let me crawl inside your skin

and whisper the words your first

love didn't know how to say

because she was eighteen

and you were twenty-two

and neither of you knew what it meant

to crave the feeling of

someone's ecstasy spread

between your fingers like drops

of Bailey's in your morning coffee

a man who knows

I need a man who knows his place—knows his hands

belong on my hips / his lips at my ear /

his name on my tongue

I need a man who knows my place—on his lap

in his bed / his shirt / his wet dreams / his poetry

I need a man who goes feral for the clack of my heels—

against marble floors / hardwood desks / glass ceilings

I need a man who deconstructs me

button by button / bow by bow / barb by barb

until he reaches / the whisper-thin skeleton of me—

the toothpick trauma / the threads that stitch

my feet to the floor

my hands in his hair / my heart on my sleeve

I need a man who tugs—draws fate to him

like a wrinkled bed sheet

like the crimson cursive of my nails on his back—

dips his knitting needle in stardust / before tying me off

I need a man comfortable in front of me and behind—

fingers splayed across my abdomen

hush, pet / burn it, baby

don't make me ask where you are

let me feel you / let me see you / let me hear you

be so very there / so very in your place

that no one ever thinks to question it

and I might just stay

I rode my fingers to sleep last night

I couldn't tell if it was agony or ecstasy, if I was pretending they were yours or trying to use my nails to claw you out of me like infected tissue. My best friend told me to put a pillow between my knees for easier access, a trick she and her husband learned while pregnant, but all I had in the guest room of my parents' house was the purple cow Squishmallow my sister bought me for my seventeenth birthday. It had never occurred to me that Mr. Moo might take the place of a man. Now I'm ashamed of what he had to take part in. I just couldn't take the ache anymore. The itching under my skin. The hummingbird heartbeat of a hunger most feral. This time, I decided not to reach for you. Like some Jungian hero destined to overcome desire, I made a mission of going it alone, letting the ghost of your voice coax me to the promised land your flesh-and-blood lips so often withheld. I determined that when I took care of myself, it would be fast and ferocious, everything your hesitation wasn't. A sure thing. A swift high. A short crash. A cracked dam that led to rushing waters that cured the valley between my thighs of its dry spell. And if the aftermath was hollow...

Well, Mr. Moo and I fell asleep before I noticed.

voyeur of joy

I float like a fish

in a rhinestone-studded bowl

cheeks sucked in a concave gasp

eyes round and glossy

at the girl on the corner / practicing a cheer routine

the receptionist humming / a headphone harmony

the left-behind streaks / of an essay well edited

the shuddering sip of steaming coffee / through soft lips

I catch pebbles of perfect

in the hollow of my throat

scaling ecstasy in a private boudoir

I'd rather be graffitied than glorified

Some women are statues,

ivory curves carved with reverent hands

by men who knew what beauty was

even if they couldn't taste its flesh.

Others are called pillars—eroded, cooled,

contracted like sickness, insanity

their only defense from buckling under burdens.

Men slap palms against our spines

with an architect's admiration—*look how*

much this column can carry. Steps whine

of being trampled on, doors scream each time

they're flayed open, and windows wish

someone would see in them, not through

them... but the pillars are holy. The pillars

are loved—and, oh, how we are envied.

Little do the laid bricks know,

pedestals get lonely.

My structure sits opposite a garden,

where stones stack themselves rough and bare.

They wear ivy like robes, show their storms

like spotted eggs, and keep wildflower

bookmarks in their cracks. They bear

the yearning of passing-through souls and serve

purpose only by happenstance.

I see them adorned with paint, crude

but never unintentional—not because a man knew

beauty proper, or grew desperate

for shelter, but because his hands demanded

to show appreciation.

box spring

you hang me from the bedpost
say I'm just for looks
hide my morning breath
inside a drawer
and button / up my tongue

you segment out / my sex appeal
save slick to soak your sheets
slide my finger bones
between your teeth
and whistle through the spores

***

I nail you to the stair rail
say I need support
dig your rotted heart
out of your chest
and plant it / in the yard

I stitch you up / in daddy's mattress
lay rose petals in a smile
record your screams
to press in vinyl
and listen for the scratches

unhinged

You unlocked the need,

then left the door wide open,

leaving me in whimpers—

yeah baby / I want him

please daddy / I need it

no worries / I promise—

to the silhouette of a ghost

lingering in the doorway,

taking the lockpick with you.

reciprocal

this isn't a situation / it's just reciprocation
the way your tongue spills secrets and I
lap them up like morning dew / between my thighs
is a keyhole and you've got the lockpick
we're just barrels and hinges / don't feign
fucking indifference

I don't need to hold your cobblestone heart in my hands
like you don't need to piss in a jar around my neck
but at least admit you watch my stories
with your hand down your pants
masturbating to my poems that aren't about you

and I come / calling to your voice when it drops
on your ex's podcast / the walls you built
are made of glass
but I've always been better from a distance

seeds of lust grow into weeds / you say
like it's a bad thing
but dandelions are pretty too / much better
for blowing wishes

tell me your boxers match my hair / I'll say
my panties match
your eyes, and when I bathe at night

it's your fingers I imagine between my thighs—
we'll trade videos
of the affair / spit-swap subliminal messages
but when your foam rolls over the rim
it's not my lips that'll be on it

you don't talk about the men
who get to watch me on stage
I don't mention the thirst traps
disguised as comments on your Substack
we both know we're pissed / you're just too proud
to admit it
because poets are piss-poor at making commitments

fine by me, baby / take your shots as you see them
just remember whose ass has you jealous of a mirror
I don't mind our threads stitching skin
instead of substance
but don't play like hyper-fixation
is a lesser erotic temptation

ask what I'm wearing / what I want / what I'd do
if I got you alone
I swear I won't say why I know what time it is
in your hometown

constrictor

here's the thing about having me

wrapped around your finger

I'm a feather boa

but my muscles coil

so if you're going to work me up,

don't forget to unwind my body

I twirled for you

In my mind, it was summer. I walked barefoot through a field of clovers, toes sinking into soil, meeting your sigh of disapproval at my too-short dress. It's grey, plain, comfortable—nothing like the ethereal champagne bubbles glittering in the flute between my fingers. We were at a wedding—a friend you admired from university and the man he loves, despite the fact that he squandered half their honeymoon fund on elaborate centerpieces. Our first outing, tinged with the promise of new horizons. You held my sandals and my heart, wondered how I could be so at ease with this much skin and soul exposed. You took my hand and spun me, watching cotton whirl around my legs like a tornado in a child's diorama. Beneath that flaring skirt were bare thighs and white lace stitched with yellow daisies. I liked the look on your face as you watched, the greed in your eyes as I spun, so I did it again and again—I teetered on tip-toes like an amateur ballerina, light as the laughter bubbling in your throat and tipsy from the tannins of you-and-me dreams that were hitting like wine, eventually scalding like tea. I made a joke about wearing wedding panties, played it off as kismet—I didn't say I bought them for you, or that I would've twirled for hours just to see you light up.

There was no wedding, and the four-leaf clover on my desk is plastic, and the video I took of storm clouds swirling at the gates of heaven died in Recently Deleted.

low blood sugar

I starved myself of love

kneeling at the foot of your table
mouth open / head back / tongue out

if I stay long enough, maybe
you'll invite me to your lap

visiting princes admire me
she looks good enough to eat, mate

I'm waiting for their hunger to rub off
on you / even the feast must be fed

I haven't seen a scrap in weeks

a Guinness in Kentucky

It shouldn't be here, this thing of darkness—
brown blood coating my throat as it closes
tight around the thickness, syrup and sap
settling in my stomach like wet soil—

It should be bourbon—I should be chasing sadness,
not sipping it… burning away
the memories, not sucking their foam
from the rim of the only thing in this bar
that bears any resemblance to you—

You shouldn't be here, this place of yearning—
clinging to me like fog held down
by the ghost of sunlight, a cold second skin
atop the sweat of a sweltering heart—

You should be underfoot—I should be dancing
on your fading pulse, not pressing my lips
against it… writing over the past,
not tapping its vein again and again
like draining this oily ichor
will turn it back to water—

I shouldn't be here, this hole of brokenness—
plastic stools sticking to cellulite thighs
bound by too-tight denim shorts, fat and fruit waiting
to fall from bone—

I should be there—I should be writhing naked in a field
of clovers, not searching for matches
to burn it... whimpering beneath your touch,
not tearing my cuticles with chipped nails
and gnashing teeth that ache at the sting of grain—

vinification

taste yourself on my tongue

lap up your promises

from the tip of my pen

and tell me the varietals

you sense on my skin

what if you'd let me

clog your pores

the way I

fermented you

in mine?

making love to nostalgia

is a dangerous game

when you forget to prune

the memories

what does your ink say

of me?

am I a ring knife

across full lips?

words bleeding

from an open slit?

drip drip

the barrel dripped ichor

but my knees stayed bruised

cork stuck between teeth

empty racks in my periphery

pressing floor getting slick

harvest shears out of reach

hair plastered purple

it's the tannins

they get to me

fist full

for you

it's a rough grip

on silky strands

the color of an enigma—

pull too hard

and the illusion might shatter

for me

it's a steady hand

on a raging bull

twitching to the touch

but shying from the chase—

work too fast

and he won't need you anymore

yeah, I swallow

Are you kidding?

Every good girl swallows.

We swallow feelings—love clots thick

like dry birthday cake / regret burns

like Tennessee whiskey / hurt curdles

like bad cream in day-old coffee—I've

been told I look pretty

choking it down.

I was already halfway gone

I knew you kept your heart in a lockbox, thought I might use the prong of your belt buckle as a key, but you didn't say the beach you buried it in was bordered by a barbed-wire fence. You only told me it was a puzzle, a typewriter set to tap out torture, but I've spun my fair share of golden tales. The problem is puzzles are meant to be put back together, but you've sharpened the edges of your shards, like a prisoner sabotaging any shot at the sun. You let her break your little heart, then warned me not to touch the pieces. Because you care for me, or because you get your kicks from erotic self-mutilation? Oh baby, we must be one and the same—my scribbles here are also razor blades. Just tell me you like it, and I won't say a word about the pretty wounds you're nursing beneath someone else's curves.

I won't even send you the burn letters I wrote.

Claire Evans (she/her) is an emerging poet and romance writer from Nashville, Tennessee, whose work balances modern eroticism with timeless lyricism. Claire's work is inspired by classic poets such as Edgar Allan Poe and William Blake, as well as newer voices like Robert Olen Butler and Richard Siken. When she's not reading or writing, Claire enjoys baking and doing jigsaw puzzles. You can find her on Instagram @thegrammarwench.

www.ingramcontent.com/pod-product-compliance
Lightning Source LLC
Chambersburg PA
CBHW020813130626
46554CB00006B/2409